Time

Poetry of an American High School Student

By Maxwell J Asciutto

Copyright ©2006 by Maxwell J Asciutto.

All rights reserved. No part of this book may be reproduced or transmitted in any form or by any means, electronic or mechanical, including photocopying, recording, or by any information storage and retrieval systems, without written permission from the author except in the case of critical articles or reviews. For information, www.ciciartist.com

Published by cici artist

Printed in the United States of America

ISBN-13: 978-0-615-13470-3

ISBN-10: 0-615-13470-X

FIRST EDITION October 2006

This collection of poetry is dedicated to my family

to my mom,
a constant support through my life

and to my sister Katie,
may we have many decades of treasured memories

with a special note to
Ms. Peck,
my poetic spark

Contents

Time	**9**
The Potion	**11**
Heart	**13**
Family Pull	**15**
What Is Love?	**19**
Stars	**23**
Perception	**29**
John C. Calhoun on Slavery in 1859	**33**
DNA	**37**
Why	**39**
Road Trip	**43**
Future Love	**47**
Notes on the Cell Phone Images	**49**
About the Author	**51**

Time

They say there is a price for everything,
I say time is the greatest price to pay,
You are a sole fighter,
Whether you are stupid or brighter,
Fatter or lighter,
You're fighting the impossible battle,
For whether you'd like to rewind, pause or fast forward,
It is no matter.
To pause the world and forever stay in the beauty of a kiss,
Or rewind to that baseball game, to that pitch,
And this time, not miss.

The Potion

Despite some hopeful notion,

There is no irresistible scent or potion,

To gain the blessing of love's devotion,

And if there were, would you dread the feeling of a non-genuine emotion?

Because you know there's only one sound of a seashell by the ocean.

Let's call it true,

That one whiff made your love interest pursue,

But to what degree would they want you?

Natural love unveils its winding course,

But how much love would beat from this source,

And would too much love delve into remorse?

Heart

Beep, beep, beep (repeat 2x, increasingly faster)
Beeeeeeeeeeeep
flat line in my heart monitor's EKG,
until you found me,
opened my heart and let my eyes see
beep beep
only way
to repay
is to express
this feeling written deep in my chest
you're like the sweet bird that taught by heart to soar from the nest
beep beep beep beep

I took a whiff of your magic potion
Riled up my strongest emotion
Filled me with an unbearable notion
That put my EKG back in motion
Beep beep beep

Feelings emerged from shadows to light
And in all fairness I don't believe in love at first sight,
Not to dispute
You've always been cute,

A friend asked me once,
If I'd ever date a girl older,
No way is what I told her
But now that it's getting colder
I just want to massage your shoulder
Because girl you make my heart beat
Bolder
Beep beep beep beep

Family Pull

For decades
Family will be there
The spark and the
Backbone to life
With love and nature's wishes
Your relationships will transcend it all
But that doesn't change the fact that
I miss you

The unquenchable need to be with you
Satisfied in the hours we are together,
The feeling returns the minute we part.

It starts small from the smile still on my face
From being with you
But the longing grows with time
And the desire only pauses
With your voice

What do I miss so much anyhow?
Kisses?
Cuddling?
Other actions I won't put in this poem?
I miss all those things

Because they're not just kisses and hugs

With you they radiate a feeling I have never felt before

Magnetic

I can feel the great pull between us

And I hope we meet in the middle

Both of us debunked from our so familiar and comfortable spots

But at least we will be rearranged together.

What Is Love?

Love is not for the weak,

Immature,

Or those who live in fear

Love is entering the unknown

Without knowing what is going to come next

Love is looking into the dark hole of fear itself
And not being afraid

For Love, is courageous

It is the ultimate care

And the ultimate trust

Love is irrational,

It doesn't make sense and it isn't part of a plan

You are drunk in love

Love is the wildest high imaginable and the greatest trip

If your lover cheats, leaves or dies,

It brings more pain than physically imaginable.

Cheating may bring the greatest hate for someone else that you never want to see again,

But at your core you still love them

Love is looking into my baby sister's sparkling eyes
As she sits on my chest and says,
"She loves me too."

Love is the journey, the test that defines who we are
And what we become

Love is the deepest of human consciousness,
"To love is to live."

Stars

"If the stars should appear but one night every thousand years how man would marvel and adore."
Ralph Waldo Emerson

Inside

Reading a magazine from the checkout line at the supermarket

Talking about the disrespectful neighbor's

While eating Breyer's ice cream after dinner

Before watching Sports Center and

Making married love for the 227th time

Inside

Only to wake in the middle of the night

With a drowsy eye to the computer screen

To skimp on sleep

To look at the internet

The window to the world

But not a 5-minute glance
Through the window to the
Universe, the
Galaxy, and the
Peaceful horizon of
Flaming Meteors,
Lit by the stars

Outside
Focus comes from the winding streetlights
That guide the driving mind
With eyes closed to the skylights
That speak to the heart

Stand outside
When darkness hugs and envelops,
You're piece of the bustling, stressful world
Bringing peace

Keep your body comfortable but point your soul to the sky
Rise
To dance with the raindrops
That are singing their natural song
Not their crash into metal rooftops
Or splat in mud puddles
But their profound voice that says
"   "

The rains speak in their accepting
Voice of peace
That welcomes their fateful
Collision with the land
In exchange for the journey through the air.

For it is a treat
To fall from the clouds

Clouds you spiral through as you rise higher
To the range of the universe that pushes down planes
And itched the minds of humans until the 1900's
How to defy that outer pull

But the strength it takes to walk submerged deep underwater
Compared with the ease of walking in air
You soar against the atmosphere
More effortlessly than any movement ever taken earth

The bustling noise of Earth is loud even
As you approach the veil of Earth and Space
And your body crosses over to space
It's as if a vacuum sucked out all the noise,
More silent and empty than the hardest sleep
You continue to rise...

In the sea of black

You hover and hang

To look back and see a tiny globe of blue and swirling wisps of white

That although you would have imagined it to be the prize object

From space

It is not

They are mesmerizing

The diamonds in the deep abyss

And although they are not forever

They are perfect

Perfect in the mega-scope

That lets us see the crystals sparkle

As you float

With no cell phone or

Watch

Your body is still

Not turning on its axis

With the chirp of midnight crickets

Or the tweet of midday birds

That fly South when the temperature changes

Or at least you seem more still than before
What is still?
Even as you hold tight on the same space coordinates
World's are spinning and orbiting
Stars are shooting and collapsing
And the moon howls from changing directions

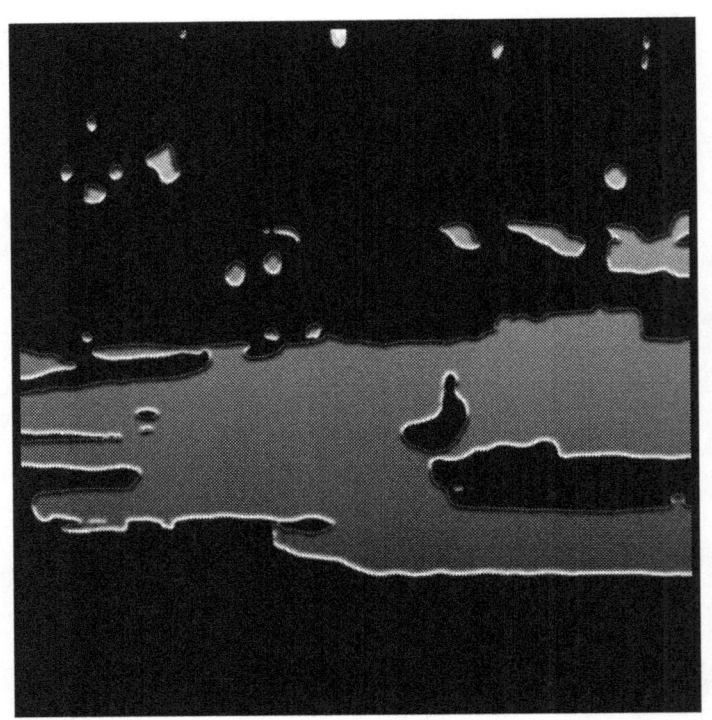

Perception

There is no career to be made in playing the lottery
We're all familiar with the echoed odds…
"One in a million"
But this world is populated with over six billion humans
And you are only one…
One in six billion

Let's shoot for the stars
And say you made $1 million dollars last year
Then you probably paid $350,000 in support of the American government
And your money was much appreciated
When it was added to the $1.9 trillion dollars the government brought in
Without you this great country would be down
. 000018421 of one percent
Without you there wouldn't be enough money for the war in Iraq
And that might be music to play on your personalized iPod
But without your generous tax dollars,
Homeland defense would be in shambles

If you feel inconsequential, at least you're special on your birthday
Twenty-four hours of glee
With your heart dancing to the melody of the birthday song
That everyone who sees you should be singing

Because out of the
365 ¼ days,
this is your day
Well....
You and the other sixteen and a half million people sharing the day that
your individuality
is treasured.

And what will your birthday bring?
Check your Yahoo! Horoscope
To find that more people are like you than you may think
In fact
With twelve signs
One out of every twelve people had the same day as you
Or 500 million of the world's six billion human's all had the same experiences
As you did.

One in twelve
You seem more unique
Than the statistics show

Only ignorance judges you by your investment in the U.S. government
And not the twelve hours a day waiting tables in three different restaurants
Or the hours you spend in the public school your parents paid for

Or the tens of thousands of dollars you took a loan out for
To pay for your higher level education
What about that?

How about the fact that your hard work at the restaurant that paid for your kids food
Will inspire their own priceless work ethic
So when your first daughter takes out a loan to pay for her own college
Her younger brother will be even more driven

And you will not be ashamed that they're paying for their own school
When they pay off their loans
And become famous
Because then you will see that all that love and hard work you put into them
Will show on the world
Where every kid growing from a minimum wage family will jump
on the little blue train
where everyone says
I think I can
I think I can
And they feel a huge surge of
Red,
White
And
Blue

When all their souls will dance with the American spirit

Even if they don't reach the fame and fortune of your kids
They will do what they love
And their happiness will attract the human love
That maneuvers through space
Making circles around the planets
That determine astrological incompatibility

John C. Calhoun on Slavery in 1859

(A representation of the South Carolinian Politician)

President, I was never elected
But like Jesus, President Buchanan has had me resurrected
Because he does not want my logical slavery views neglected
To keep this great countries union protected

We in the South look to preserve our peace
And ask for the radical abolition movement
to cease
For the aristocratic and working class divide has been successful since the days of Ancient Greece
Alas,
Every successful and civilized society has had more wealth in the non-producing class,

Any man can pound a nail into wood pine
But only the intelligent can guide the design
And as you know,
The white man is America's true backbone and spine,
As we in the south feel it is time
To put the radical abolition movement
Back in line

Any man can pick cotton and stick it in a bag,
But the intelligent whites are the only ones to guide the wave of our American flag,

Where the black people should not look on our relationship as a drag,
For it is no mystery,
That in all African people's history,
Their conditions here are the best they have ever, ever
Lived under
With their cross-Atlantic journeys anything but a blunder,
But they have missed the benefit of our white lightning,
And only shudder at our unrelated thunder

For no more,
Do the African Americans worry about tribal war,
No worries of famine with food always in store,
And the blessings of Jesus right at their door.

Life on a Southern plantation
Is the black's first and greatest source of civilization
A collaboration
Of white influence through daily association
And black acceptance of their obligation
To be a part of our great nation
They should show appreciation
For America lending its hand in their organization

A sick Southern slave is looked after with care,
With his master and mistress looking after him like a whiff of good air,
While the life of a sick pauper in any European country cannot compare,

As their poor life dangles by a hair,
No house takes them in,
They are left out cold and bare
In lonely and dying solitaire
While the slave sits in a comfortable chair
And hears the word of his family and mistress in prayer

To conclude,
Our gentlemen institution of slavery and peace we do adore,
We simply ask to keep the blacks on their chore,
But stir the Southern lion,
And hear our roar
Like mother Earth we keep fire in our core

Please do not hear my word with one ear,
But listen,
If you care to keep our great country from cession,
And continue the mission
To quickly close down this mislead movement of abolition.

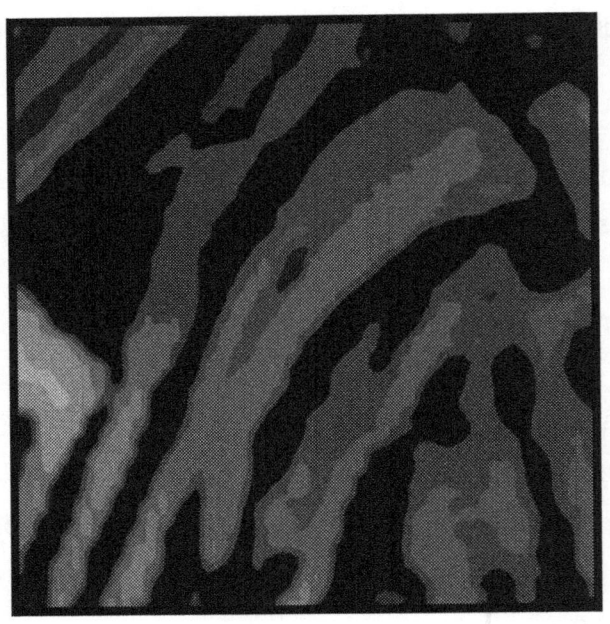

DNA

Fiery Earth burning at its core,
It's crackle emits an "AHH" scream
Like men asking to be pulled up
From the hole that is death
And their screams are answered by a clear fog
That fills lungs like an ice pad on a burning forehead
And
Jumpstarts hearts
to catch the beat to finish the music
They thought they would never get to play

Like leaves being blown from Fall trees
They imagined their being, their self,
Making a slow and gentle fall
Into peace
And just as they had grown from a great combination of the
Earth's minerals, collaborating to form
The great code,
The great key,
To
Life
Life that would one day return the favor
To not so much deteriorate
As be rearranged into thousands of peaceful pieces
Like parmesan cheese grinded to flavor the most delicious of
Pizzas

Why

Face flushed with white heat,
As my rib cage
Takes a pounding from my fast and furious heart beat
His hand is clenching my heart

Watched
Two unwanted eyes on me
What is he looking at?
What does he went?
I have no money,
Doesn't he know that!?
Only thing valuable I have is my cell phone,
Cell phone!
I'll call
O shit it's dead

I've heard of being followed
But what about being lead?
He is ahead of me
And stares back
He's strolling at an uncomforting pace
And the faster I go
The closer he comes

This is only my second time in this town
And I know no other way to the midnight train
No time to run back
What If I turn down one of the quiet road?
Wait, and then he'll be gone
But what if he follows?
Then I'm stuck on a dark ambiguous street

He's looking again,
He is waving violently
I slow down a bit
But the slower I go the faster he signals
Signals!?
My neck contours to the bent arm of a sweatshirt
My eyes open wider
Than my SCREA-
Cotton covers my mouth

With adrenaline pumping
I have to fight back!
A quick push and shove
But once he gets handle

My dead body and murderer are shrinking to a speck
As I look down from my rising soul
This is a great feeling

Transcending all those earthly limitations that bound me for so many years

And I soar

On my way back home

I feel like I'm slowing down in the stratosphere

My knees buckle

Onto a movie seat?

I look around

It's like I'm on the inside of a giant ring

With movie screens circling

Ten scenes playing simultaneously

And I'm living and comprehending them all

That's because I did live them!

It's my last life!

Oh that was a good time with the family!

I'll miss them...

But the memories are getting darker

The screen goes black as the room goes pitch

And as I look down

I can't even see my hands

Three flashes of light

And the black screens connect with one drawn out word

"Why?"

Road Trip

Life is like a flowing river
F- that and give it the scissor
And while you're at it
Cut the omniscient responsibilities
The family,
The school,
The homework,
The tests,
Laborious hours at work
And the stress
No picking out your clothes
No one here cares how you dress
Put down the worn out pitching forked keyboard
Drop the overalls and tell Dad we're leaving the farm
On the way out
Skin the feathers off the sun-rise rooster
And mute the screeching morning alarm

Forget the everyday
With each hour planned
Just duck now when shit hits the fan
Stay calm and be prepared for heart pumping danger
Keep your eyes focused on curves of the road
With ears pitched to hear the sirens of the Texas Ranger

Yellow dashes whizzing by
Cars choking in our dust, think we can fly
Radar eyes on the badged magnum
Tell your boys in the back to pass the dragon
Keep your head up and the wheels spinning on the wagon
Reflect on the perky and highlight what's sagging

You may get dizzy
And begin to fall
When the road over-twists
Under dreary eyes
As time passes
Have no fear your closest friends are here
To remind you that you are no longer held down by the masses
Experience and companionship
To defog your convoluted glasses
To bring you up higher than before
To off the goggles and walk confidently with laser eyes surgery allure
No longer are the unknown roads a chore

Close friends all huddled up
Fizz in our stomachs
Magic in our mind
Hope in our heart

And Mel Gibson in our lungs,
"FREEEDOOOM!!"
Heard on the ladder of life,
At the highest rungs

Windows down
As you sip the calm breeze
And chew on the waving branches of palm trees
When you see that friend down and crying
Tell them to get off their knees
Cuz we're searching for Shangri-La
Our bodies on the paved road
And souls in the blue seas
Where ideas shine on colorful corals
Time to lose societal influence and explore morals
They say,
"Do what's right
And fight the evil!"
But who draws those pearly lines?
And anyway what is true?
Only way to find out is to stir the stew,
Ignore all outsourced ideas,
And see the road
For what it means to you.

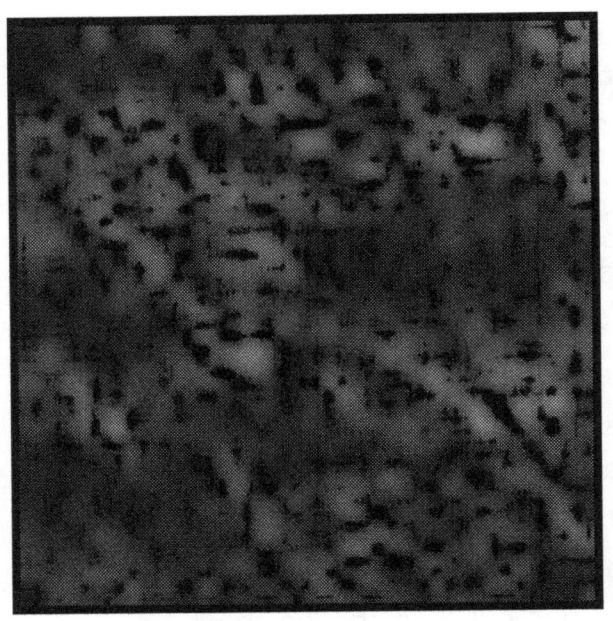

Future Love

This modern day leaves us with the age-old prism
That even in this American world of capitalism
Where it seems everything can be found with a shopping cart
My continuous search for the one to fill my heart
Flirts with the one, but always circles back to the start
Only time holds the key
Who will she be?

I wish I could TiVo life, and fast forward the tape
And find the one who fills my dreams with her indefinite shape
When I wake in the night at whom will my eyes stare?
Is she a brunette, a blonde, or does she have sweet red hair?
No matter her colorings I don't care
A lawyer, a writer, a waitress, an entrepreneur or a biologist
What will be her greatest interest?
As the thought of her leaves me impressed,
I ponder the qualities that will skip a beat in my chest.

Whatever the case
I promise an eternity of grace
As my arms spread wide open for embrace
I'd give anything now for one glance at her face.

Notes on the Cell Phone Images

We are all inclined to particular skills, and although I have the utmost respect for the art of photography, my pull to it is weak. I cannot compete with snap-shot enthusiast and with that knowledge I did something different. The pictures were shot from my low-resolution camera phone, cropped, and edited in Adobe Photoshop for a mark of style.

original photographs:

cropped images:

About the Author

Maxwell Asciutto was inspired to write poetry in Miss. Peck's inspirational Writers Workshop class.

This is his first publication of his poetry written predominantly while a junior in high school, both in and out of class.

www.ingramcontent.com/pod-product-compliance
Lightning Source LLC
Chambersburg PA
CBHW051719040426
42446CB00008B/957